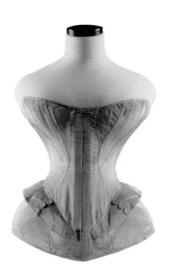

Published in 2013 by The Rosen Publishing Group, Inc.
29 East 21st Street, New York, NY 10010

Photo Credits: **KEY** tl=top left; tc=top center; tr=top right; cl=center left; c=center; cr=center right; bl=bottom left; bc=bottom center; br=bottom right; bg=background
CBT = Corbis; GI = Getty Images; iS = istockphoto.com; PDCD = PhotoDisc; SH = Shutterstock; TF = Topfoto; TPL = photolibrary.com
front cover SH; **1**c TF; **2–3**bg iS; tc TF; **4**bg PDCD; c TPL; **5**bg PDCD; **6**c, cl, cr, tr TF; **6–7**c TF; **7**c, cr, tr TF; TPL; **8**tr TPL; **8–9**bg PDCD; tr TF; **9**br TF; **10**bc, br TF; tl TPL; **10–11**bg iS; c TF; **11**c CBT; **12**tr CBT; bc SH; **12–13**bg PDCD; **13**tr SH; **14**tr TF; **14–15**bg iS; bl TF; **15**tr iS; br, cr, cr, tl TF; **16**bl, tr TF; **16–17**bg iS; **17**bl, cr, tl TF; **18**tc TF; **18–19**bg iS; **19**br, cl TF; **20**c TF; **20–21**bg iS; tc TF; **21**br, c TF; **22–23**bg iS; c TF; **23**bc, c TF; **24**bl TF; **24–25**bg iS; br, tc TF; **25**tc iS; tc, tr TF; **26**cl iS; br TF; **27**c TPL; **28**br GI; tr iS; bl SH; **29**bl iS; cr, tl SH; tr TPL; **30–31**bg iS; **31**c TF; **32**bg iS

All illustrations copyright Weldon Owen Pty Ltd. **8**br, **13**br, **19**t Andrew Davies/Creative Communication

Weldon Owen Pty Ltd
Managing Director: Kay Scarlett
Creative Director: Sue Burk
Publisher: Helen Bateman
Senior Vice President, International Sales: Stuart Laurence
Vice President Sales North America: Ellen Towell
Administration Manager, International Sales: Kristine Ravn

Library of Congress Cataloging-in-Publication Data

Park, Louise, 1961–
 Extreme fashions / by Louise Park.
   p. cm. — (Discovery education: sensational true stories)
 Includes index.
 ISBN 978-1-4777-0061-7 (library binding) — ISBN 978-1-4777-0107-2 (pbk.) —
 ISBN 978-1-4777-0108-9 (6-pack)
 1. Fashion—History—Juvenile literature. 2. Beauty, Personal—History—Juvenile literature. I. Title.
 GT518.P35 2013
 391--dc23
                                                        2012019587

Manufactured in the United States of America

CPSIA Compliance Information: Batch #W13PK2 : For Further Information contact Rosen Publishing, New York, New York at 1-800-237-9932

SENSATIONAL TRUE STORIES

EXTREME FASHIONS

LOUISE PARK

PowerKiDS
press.

New York

Contents

Time Line of Fashions

Men and women have always been drawn to fashion, and it has been used to define social class, tribal belonging, and historical periods. It includes clothing, footwear, hairstyles, makeup, jewelry, and body adornment and reshaping.

Not all fashion has been sensible, practical, or safe. In fact, some trends have been unhealthy, dangerous, and even fatal. This book looks at the trends from long ago to the present. It shows what people wore and did to keep up with the fashions of the day. Which fashions seem extreme to you?

3700 BC
Lip plates and earplugs made of fired clay or wood are ancient forms of body adornment. They are still worn by certain tribes around the world today.

AD 800s
In China, the feet of wealthy women were tightly bound to make them smaller and in the shape of a lotus flower. This practice continued until the early 1900s.

1000s
Tribes in Myanmar and South Africa have been wearing neck rings for thousands of years. The tradition continues today among certain tribes in those regions.

1100s
Europe was exposed to new fashion ideas, styles, and fabrics because of trade with Asia and the Middle East. This period is often referred to as the Fashion Explosion.

1400s
Men's fashion became colorful, flamboyant, and extravagant. Men wore vivid tights, starched neck ruffs, high-heeled shoes, jeweled garters, codpieces, and more.

1500s
The corset began its tight grip on the waistlines of women in the early 1500s. It evolved from an iron corset, and went in and out of fashion for the next four centuries.

1600s
Fontanges appeared in the late 1600s. These very high hairdos that included wire, sculptures, feathers, ribbons, and jewels were the cause of many fashion disasters.

1800s
Wearing a crinoline cage under a dress made the skirt part of the dress fan out around the body. Some crinoline cages were so wide that women got caught in doorways.

Lip and Ear Plates

Lip and ear plates, also called plugs or disks, are used by a number of tribes around the world. Once worn by both women and men, they are now almost exclusively worn by women. As well as being body adornments, lip plates symbolize a woman's strength, maturity, and social status.

Lip and ear plates are now used mainly by the Mursi, Chai, and Tirma peoples in Africa. When a girl is around 15 or 16 years old, her mother or another woman from her settlement cuts her lip. A wooden plug is then inserted in the cut to hold it open while it heals. Ever-larger plates are inserted over the months. Ears are pierced and the holes gradually enlarged in a similar way.

Decorative plate
Lip plates vary from tribe to tribe, but most of them are made from wood or clay. Many women take pride in carving the plates and decorating them with intricate designs.

POPULAR AMONG MANY TRIBES

Lip and ear plates are still used by the Mursi, Chai, and Tirma peoples in Ethiopia and by Suyá men in Brazil. Up until only a few decades ago, the Sara women of Chad, the Makonde of Tanzania and Mozambique, and the Botocudo of Brazil also wore them. The Inuit, Aleut, and other indigenous peoples of Alaska and northern Canada used lip plates until the end of the nineteenth century.

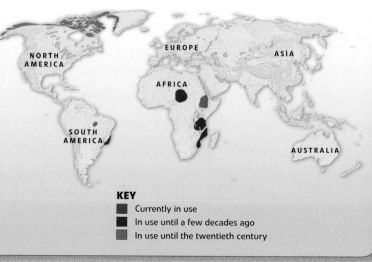

KEY
- Currently in use
- In use until a few decades ago
- In use until the twentieth century

Stretching the lips

These Makonde women in Tanzania have had their lips stretched by progressively larger lip plates. Once the first cut heals, the first plate is replaced by a bigger plate, which stretches the lip even more. This continues over several months. Some women's lips can hold a plate larger than 4 to 5 inches (10 to 12.5 cm) across. Often, their four front teeth have to be removed to make space for the plate.

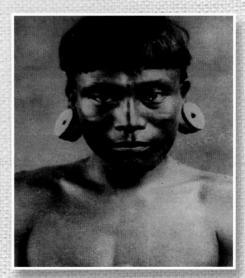

The Wooden Ears
The people of one tribe of the Amazon rain forest in Brazil are known as Wooden Ears because they elongate their earlobes with ear plates. Boys' ears are pierced in a ritual when they are 14 or 15 years old.

That's Amazing!

The lip plate has been invented independently as many as six times in different places around the world. Each tribe developed their own style of plate.

Chinese Foot Binding

The practice of foot binding is thought to have begun in China during the ninth century, when a woman with bound feet performed a dance for the ruler of the time. Other dancers were so captivated by her tiny bound feet, they began binding their own in cloth to make them appear smaller. Soon, the idea of having small feet became the desire of almost all women. Girls from three to fourteen years old had their feet bound. The aim was to break the foot arch and curve it into the shape of a lotus flower 3 to 4 inches (7.5 to 10 cm) long. This painful process was repeated day and night until the feet stopped growing and set in the new shape. It made walking difficult and running almost impossible.

A sign of wealth
Women with bound feet often had to be carried around by servants, so foot binding was seen as a mark of wealth in the middle and upper classes.

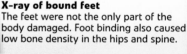

Tiny shoes
Shoes were specially made for women who had bound feet. The shoes were slender and pointy like a triangle to fit the size and shape of the deformed foot.

THE BINDING PROCESS

Binding was done with a piece of cloth that was about 10 feet (3 m) long and 2 inches (5 cm) wide. The toenails were trimmed away almost completely to prevent them from growing into the flesh of the foot. Tight wrapping of the cloth around the foot caused the bones to move around in the foot until the arch bones broke, then mended in a new shape. The toes then curled under the ball of the foot.

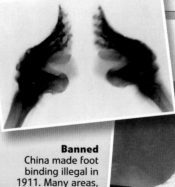

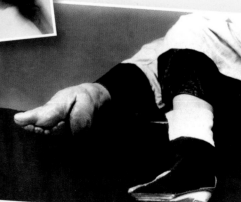

X-ray of bound feet
The feet were not the only part of the body damaged. Foot binding also caused low bone density in the hips and spine.

Banned
China made foot binding illegal in 1911. Many areas, especially remote rural ones, ignored this. The practice was eradicated in 1949.

The price of fashion

Bound feet, like the feet of these women, may have been desirable, but it was not always successful. Many women suffered gangrene because their feet would get infected. It was quite common for women to lose their toes in the process. Some women even lost their feet.

Men liked bound feet so much that it became a privilege for them to see a foot unbound.

Neck Rings

The women of the Padaung tribes in Myanmar (Burma) and the Ndebele people in South Africa wear neck rings to create the illusion of having a long and slender neck. The Padaung start the process when a girl turns five or six years old, and a brass ring is added every passing year. Women can eventually have up to 37 neck rings around their neck. The rings reach from the clavicle, or collarbone, to beneath the chin.

Ndebele women tend to wear neck rings after marriage. Copper and brass rings around the neck, arms, and legs of a married woman symbolize a bond of faithfulness to her husband.

Why Padaung women wear neck rings
According to Padaung mythology, women wear neck rings to stop tigers from biting them. However, the most common explanation is that neck rings and a long neck are signs of beauty and wealth, and women with rings will attract a better husband than those without rings.

How neck rings work
Neck rings are worn from a young age but do not actually make the neck longer. The weight of the copper rings pushes down on the collarbones and the upper ribs to give an illusion of a longer neck. The rings push at such an angle that the collarbones seem to be part of the neck.

The copper and brass rings often leave a stain on the skin similar to a bruise.

The side effects
Neck rings do not pose any great danger to their wearers. However, the rings do leave bruising and they can often be painful to remove. The rings also weaken the neck muscles, leaving wearers with smaller and more fragile necks than other women.

WHERE IN THE WORLD

The Padaung people occupy one of the states in the central part of Myanmar. A small number of Padaung tribes also live in the Mae Hong Son province of northwest Thailand and are often referred to as the Kayan. There are two groups of Ndebele people in South Africa, the Mpumalanga Ndebele and the North Ndebele. The different groups are separated by Springbok Flats.

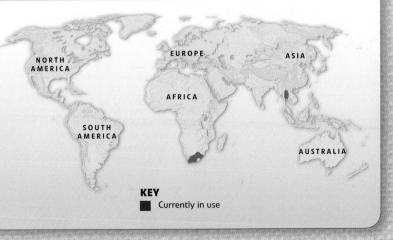

NORTH AMERICA

EUROPE

ASIA

AFRICA

SOUTH AMERICA

AUSTRALIA

KEY
■ Currently in use

Trends of the 1100s and 1200s

Exploration and travel opened up more parts of the world. Some people traveled to places such as Russia and the Middle East, or met merchants from Asia. Gradually, new materials and styles made their way back to Europe.

Clothes were expensive. There were no sewing machines, so all clothes had to be sewed by hand. Fashion became a sign of class and wealth as a result. Royalty and nobles decided what was fashionable, and ordinary people tried to copy them.

Influence of the Crusades
The Crusades were European military campaigns in the Middle East. They brought Europeans into contact with many different cultures. They began to imitate the fashions of these new places and import new textiles, such as silk, satin, velvet, and brocades.

Long or short tunics
Men wore inner tunics or shirts with long sleeves, and leggings known as hose. Outer tunics fell to the knees or ankles and were pulled in at the waist with a belt. Longer outer tunics were worn only by noblemen at court. They were not for riding or fighting. Being a warrior, King Henry II of England usually preferred the shorter, more practical tunic, but is seen here wearing a long outer tunic.

Headwear of the time

Headwear was simple for both men and women during the medieval period in England and France, and fashions in headwear were slow to change.

The first hats were hoods—some were tied under the chin. Round caps with a small brim followed. They had a tab at the top and some looked a little like the French beret of today.

Hoods

Caps

Courtiers

Courtiers were people who attended the royal court and were either from noble families or intellectuals. The latest trends and newest fashions were most obvious among these courtiers because they could afford them.

ARTISANS

Artisans were people who worked in a particular trade. As western Europe came into contact with the Middle East and Asia, European artisans and craftspeople began to form an important part of society. Some were regarded more highly than others, particularly tailors, who sewed high fashion, shoemakers, and jewelers.

Medieval artisans at work

Men's Fashion

Women were not the only ones attracted to fashion excess. In the fifteenth to seventeenth centuries, men wore frills, furs, movement-restricting garments, lace, jewels, makeup, and high heels. Tights were the fundamental fashion item. Initially, they were two separate stockings made of wool or cloth, which were attached to the bottom of tunics or breeches with laces. When knitted fabric started being produced, tights became very fitted and men showed off their shapely legs in fancy colors, stripes, and patterns. Garters were a fashionable way to keep tights up. Many were decorated in jewels, velvet, silk, and ribbons.

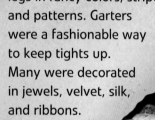

Doublets and breeches
In the late sixteenth century, men followed the fashions of Spain. Doublets were close-fitting buttoned jackets, thickly padded at this time. Breeches were also padded around the thighs and known as bombasted breeches.

Louis XIV of France
King Louis XIV (1638–1715) was one of the most fashion-obsessed kings of all. He wore coats of silver and gold and was never seen without silk stockings. He also started the trend of high-heeled shoes for men. Today, a high, curved heel is called the Louis heel.

Neck ruffs and skirt breeches

Men wore starched neck ruffs that fanned out stiffly from the neck like a cartwheel. Wrist ruffs were also popular. Short, wide upper breeches, or hose, were stuffed with padding and looked almost like short skirts.

That's Amazing!

A peascod was a doublet that had been stuffed with wool or sawdust to create an extreme potbellied shape, like a stomach paunch. It was also called an artificial potbelly.

Henry VIII of England

Under the Sumptuary Laws, only royalty could have access to certain fashion items. King Henry VIII, his close family, and his courtiers were the only people in England who were allowed to wear purple silk, cloth of gold, and certain furs.

Earl of Surrey wearing a codpiece *c.* 1550

CODPIECES

Tights were two separate stockings, which left a gap between the legs. A codpiece filled that gap. Originally just concealing flaps of cloth, codpieces became one of the more spectacular fashion accessories of the time. They were adorned with ribbons and jewels and puffed out past other clothing.

The Corset

The corset was a garment worn to shape and mold the torso. It narrowed the waistline and accentuated the bust and hips. Women began wearing corsets in the 1500s, when Catherine de Médicis, wife of King Henry II of France, banned thick waists in the French court.

Corsets were made of cloth, leather, or iron, with strips of whalebone or sometimes metal inserted in the seams. They were done up with laces, which were pulled so tight that the size of a woman's waist could be reduced by one third or more. Corsets were rigid and uncomfortable to wear. They went in and out of fashion for 400 years.

The hourglass figure

The early 1900s saw a revival of old-style corsets that pulled in the waistline. Corsets with whalebone reinforcements that laced up at the front for convenience encased the torso. They squeezed the waist to new extremes to create the famous hourglass figure. Women were laced so tight that they needed help to get dressed for the day.

That's Amazing!

One of the corsets worn by Catherine de Médicis was made of iron. It was said that the corset kept her waist pulled in so tight, it measured a tiny 13 inches (33 cm) around.

DANGEROUSLY TIGHT

Tightly laced corsets constricted the ribs and forced them downward, putting pressure on organs such as the ovaries. As a result, some women could not become pregnant. If corsets were laced too tightly, a woman's lungs could become overinflated and she might even start bleeding internally. Corsets restricted movement and breathing, which made it impossible to do any form of exercise. Digesting food was difficult, too.

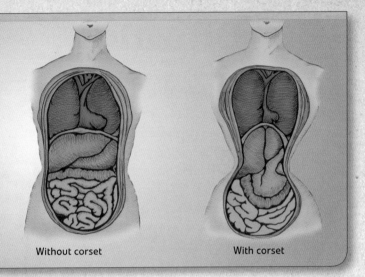

Without corset   With corset

Princesses Victoria and Maud of England
The princesses' tiny waists were achieved with extremely tight lacing of their corsets. Tight corsets restricted almost every type of activity. Doctors warned that pressure from corsets would damage and dislocate women's internal organs, but fashion usually won out over safety.

The longer line corset
Undergarments that built up the bust and cinched the waist to create an hourglass shape were desired by every woman in the early 1900s. An elongated corset that laced down the torso and over the hips was used to achieve this shape.

The Fontange

Fashion in hairstyles reached a high point during the seventeenth century with the emergence of the fontange, a very tall hairdo, like a tower. The fontange was named after Mademoiselle de Fontanges, one of French King Louis XIV's girlfriends. Her hair became very messy on a hunting trip, so she tied it up with a garter, or ribbon. The king thought she looked so stunning that he asked her to always wear her hair up. Every lady of the court copied her and a new hairstyle was born.

Reaching new heights

Women wore elaborate constructions more than 8 inches (20 cm) high, made from layers of pleated ruffles held up with wire. The highest of all fontanges was worn by the Duchess of Devonshire, in England. It was a sculpted tower more than 47 inches (1.2 m) high that took two hairdressers hours to erect.

Hair panoramas
Famous hairdressers created extravagant designs with ostrich feathers, model carriages, fruits, vegetables, and even flowers with water wells. These designs were modeled to fit around the skull.

Expensive styles
This was an expensive and time-consuming hairstyle, so women would keep the same style for weeks. The elaborate constructions became hot, heavy, and very itchy, and women used head-scratchers to relieve their itching scalps. Their hair was powdered with flour and starch. It attracted lice, insects, spiders, and even, it is said, mice.

That's Amazing!
Fontanges grew so tall that they regularly caught fire on the candles in chandeliers. They made walking difficult, and any quick movement was virtually impossible.

TOO HIGH FOR COMFORT

The fontange was very popular throughout Europe from the 1680s to the early 1700s. During this time, women tried to outdo each other with more elaborate styles and headdress heights. Some styles were so high and heavy that their owners needed servants to walk behind them to hold up their hairdo with a stick. This prevented the towering hairdo from toppling over.

Lead Makeup

The desire for pale skin has existed through the ages, but the most dangerous product used to achieve it was lead face paint, or lead makeup. This was a cream made from vinegar, egg whites, and powdered white lead—a deadly ingredient that caused lead poisoning.

Mild lead poisoning would result in nausea, stomach pain, and headaches. Severe lead poisoning caused insanity and even death. When painted on the face, the cream gave off a shiny appearance. Wearers could not smile very much because smiling made the paint crack. The cream also caused scarring on some skin.

Queen Elizabeth I

Elizabeth I of England started the trend of using lead face paint. She used it to hide the scars she had after contracting smallpox, and was obsessed with having a perfectly white face. Although there was no postmortem done on her body, many believe the constant application of lead gave her blood poisoning, which eventually killed her.

That's Amazing!

Lead makeup had such high poison levels that it eroded women's eyebrows and the hair at the hairline. It also infected their skin, which only encouraged them to use more.

In the name of beauty

Lead makeup was very fashionable during the seventeenth and eighteenth centuries. In the mid-1700s, two of the most beautiful women in England were Maria Gunning, Countess of Coventry, and Catherine Marie Fisher, a courtesan. Both wore lead-based makeup and vied for the love of George William, Earl of Coventry. Maria Gunning was to eventually marry him, while Catherine Fisher married a member of parliament, John Norris. Both women died young from blood poisoning caused by exposure to the lead in their makeup.

Maria Gunning
The Earl of Coventry's wife, Maria Gunning, was said to have disliked her honeymoon because her husband would not let her wear lead makeup. She died when she was 27.

Catherine "Kitty" Fisher
Catherine Fisher was one of the most renowned English beauties of the time. She died in 1767, only four months after her marriage to John Norris.

The Crinoline Cage

During the early 1800s, people wove horsehair into linen to make a fabric called crinoline. This was used to make stiff petticoats, which pushed out the skirt of a dress so that it appeared fuller. By 1855, a woman was expected to have at least six petticoats under her dress or she would be thought unfashionable and inappropriately dressed. However, wearing so many stiff petticoats weighed a great deal, and they were dangerously hot during summer. In 1856, an invention called the crinoline cage solved this problem.

Framework
The traditional crinoline cage had a frame of flexible steel hoops. Vertical strips of tape held the hoops together. Women needed to wear only the cage and one petticoat. They were no longer weighed down by several layers of hot, heavy petticoat and could now move their legs freely beneath the cage.

A FATAL FASHION DEVICE

Crinoline cages had some problems. Skirts that flared out to cumbersome widths were very difficult to sit down in. Women often had difficulty fitting through doorways that were not wide enough for their skirts, or got stuck. In 1863, about 1,800 women died when a church in Santiago, Chile, caught fire. In the rush to get out, the women's crinoline cages blocked the exit. They were trapped and burned to death.

The "La Compañia" church in Chile that burned down in 1863.

All shapes and sizes
Crinoline cages and bustles came in all shapes and sizes. Some were pyramid-shaped, some round. Some extended only the back of the dress. Nearly all the dresses with attachments were heavy to wear as they consisted of yards and yards of fabric, frills, bows, and bustles, and could weigh up to 22 pounds (10 kg).

The tournure

By about 1869, the tournure dress improver, also known as the bustle, had replaced the crinoline cage. The tournure consisted of a small frame, or bustle, made of narrow steel and tapes. This had several layers of flounced horsehair, which were all bunched at the back of the tournure. It was tied at the waist and a petticoat of white brilliantine was attached over the top. This created fullness at the back of a dress from the waist down.

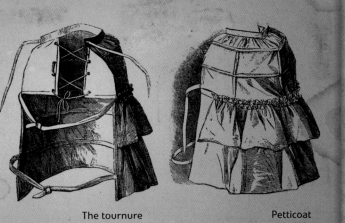

The tournure   Petticoat

New Heights

High-heeled shoes raise the heel higher than the toes. They give the illusion of a longer and more slender leg, and they also make the wearer taller. Shoes with platforms date back to the ancient Egyptians, but high-heeled shoes as a fashion item first appeared during the 1500s, when two prominent royals wanted to appear taller.

Catherine de Médicis, married to King Henry II of France, was not quite 5 feet (1.5 m) tall. She wore shoes with heels 2 inches (5 cm) high to raise her height. King Louis XIV of France wore intricate heels up to 5 inches (12.5 cm) high to compensate for being short.

That's Amazing!

King Louis XIV made a ruling that no one's heels could be higher than his and that only noblemen and noblewomen could wear shoes with a red heel.

High-heeled shoes
Today, high heels are mostly worn by women and can vary in height from 1 inch (2.5 cm) to extreme heights of 5 inches (12.5 cm) or more. Although high heels can be flattering, they can also be harmful for the wearer. They cause foot pain and change the natural angles of the foot and leg. They increase the risk of sprains and fractures and can affect the knee joint.

CARMEN MIRANDA

At the peak of her career as a singer and actress in the 1940s, Carmen Miranda was the highest paid woman in Hollywood. She inspired many fashion trends with her flamboyant dress sense. She was known for her colorful outfits and her headgear decorated with fruit. She is also credited with starting the trend for high-heeled platform shoes and had an enormous collection of them.

Adding inches
Carmen Miranda was only 5 feet 3 inches (1.6 m) tall and wore platforms for extra height.

Platform shoes

Geta sandals or clogs are traditional Japanese platform shoes, and the Turks wore a similar style in the 1700s. Two wooden blocks raise the toe and heel equally; another piece of wood forms the sole. Some are dangerously high and very difficult to walk in. People need plenty of practice before they can walk safely in even a moderately high pair of platform shoes.

Fashion Today

Fashion has come a long way from fire-catching fontanges, door-blocking crinoline cages, and rib-crushing corsets, but even some of today's trends can cause harm to their wearers. The everyday items on this page might look trendy and seem innocent enough, but their potential to harm or cause ill health is real.

Long scarves

Long scarves keep the neck warm, but they get caught in all sorts of things from escalators to cars. The famous US dancer Isadora Duncan died in 1927 when her long scarf got caught in a moving wheel of an open-topped car.

Heavy bags

Oversized bags can fit many items inside, but their weight can cause neck, shoulder, and back pain. Physiotherapists and chiropractors warn that carrying a heavy bag has a damaging effect on the body, which occurs gradually and increases over time.

Pointy shoes

High-heeled shoes with pointy toes compress the toes and feet. The heels put pressure on the five long bones in the foot called the metatarsal bones. The point constricts the toes, causing foot pain and possibly bunions.

Contact lenses

Doctors warn of the dangers of using nonprescription "fashion lenses." These are colored contact lenses that do not improve vision but simply change the color or appearance of the eyes. They can cause infections on the corneas' surface, threatening a person's sight.

Tight jeans

Tight, stretchy jeans are popular but can be a health risk. Too-tight jeans can cause tingling-thigh syndrome, which affects the nerves in the outer region of the thigh and causes numbness, hypersensitivity, and a burning sensation.

Dangling earrings

Long, dangling, or heavy earrings or huge hoops can damage the earlobes. Earrings can weigh the lobe down and cause it to stretch. They can also get caught in things and pulled, and this may tear the earlobe. Just brushing your hair could do this.

Chemicals and dyes

Certain synthetic fabrics, including fake leather and some waterproof clothing, contain chemicals that can be harmful. These fabrics can release chemicals and toxic fumes. Synthetic fabric dyes also contain chemicals that can be harmful. Natural dyes are a safer choice.

Glossary

bone density
(BOHN DEN-seh-tee)
A measurement of the amount of bone tissue in a specified volume of bone. Poor bone density is linked to higher fracture risk.

brilliantine (BRIL-yen-teen)
A dress fabric made from cotton and mohair.

brocades (bro-KAYDZ)
Rich fabrics that have a flamboyant pattern raised on them, typically in gold or silver thread.

compensate (KOM-pen-sayt)
To make up for something or reimburse for a loss.

corneas (KOR-nee-ahz)
The parts of the eyes covering the pupils.

courtesan (KOR-tuh-zin)
A woman courtier who attended the courts of the royals.

courtiers (KOR-tee-urz)
People who attend the court of a king or royal.

cumbersome (KUM-ber-sum)
Troublesome or clumsy.

dislocate (DIHS-loh-kayt)
To put out of place or position.

eroded (ih-ROHD-ed)
Slowly eaten into or eaten away at.

flamboyant (flam-BOY-ent)
Bold or strikingly brilliant.

flounced (FLOWNSD) Built out by having wide ruffles sewn into its skirt.

gangrene (GANG-green)
A disease that kills skin as a result of very poor circulation.

hypersensitivity
(hy-per-sen-sih-TIV-ih-tee)
Extreme sensitivity to something.

insanity (in-SAH-nih-tee)
Senselessness in the mind.

lotus flower
(LOH-tus FLOW-er) A pink flower native to India.

mythology
(mih-THAH-luh-jee) A collection of fictional stories or myths of a specific society, often dealing with heroes, ancestors, or supernatural beings.

nausea (NAW-zhee-uh)
Sickness in the stomach.

nobles (NOH-bulz)
People distinguished by rank or title.

postmortem
(pohst-MOR-tum) Surgery after death on a body to determine cause of death.

ritual (RIH-choo-ul)
An activity performed regularly, often religious in nature.

sprains (SPRAYNZ)
Stretched and damaged
ligaments and tendons.

synthetic (sin-THEH-tik)
Not natural; artificially created.

textiles (TEK-stylz)
Cloths made by knitting,
weaving, sewing, or felting.

torso (TOR-soh) The top half
of the body, from the neck to
the waist.

Index

Websites

Due to the changing nature of Internet links, PowerKids Press has developed an online list of websites related to the subject of this book. This site is updated regularly. Please use this link to access the list: www.powerkidslinks.com/disc/xfash/